WHICH LIES ARE NECESSARY?

WHICH LIES ARE NECESSARY?

A Chapbook

Ann Humphreys

Hollyridge Press
Venice, California

© 2005 Ann Humphreys

All rights reserved under International and Pan-American Copyright Conventions. Published in the United States by Hollyridge Press.

Hollyridge Press
P.O. Box 2872
Venice, California 90294
www.hollyridgepress.com

Cover and Book Design by Rio Smyth
Author photo by Bill Bamberger
Manufactured in the United States of America by Lightning Source

ISBN-13: 978-0-9752573-7-1
ISBN-10: 0-9752573-7-4

Contents

One
Back in the 90s	3
February	4
Those Were the Days	5
The Way To Do It	6
Country Club	7
Reception	9
Lost Song	10
Pick a Scene	11
1985	12
Summer Holiday	13
89.3	14
Celebrity	16
August	17
Stork	18
A Month of Mondays	19
Stripper	20
Veil	21
Holidays	22
Christmas Day	23

Two
Independence Day, 2002	27
Lesson in Adulthood	28
Sue Ann Court	29
Reflections in a Blue Eye	30
Notice	31
Jealousy	32
Superstar	33
Aisle	34
Jesus Stops In	35
Hope	36

One

BACK IN THE 90S

We cannot go back to the life
of bike transport and pool pirating,
of Missy popping open a Blackened Voodoo
chirping vegan recipes while her hands
flew spindles over the silverware, perched
like a bird in her tight-waisted 40s dresses.

Long past Mary, or Shay,
stabbing out Marlboros in the side room
to chunk across the lino tile in big shoes
towards the side work that took me
45 minutes to their 15, we sit
in adulthood that comes so easily.

Never again such a long summer, days ironed in
between epic nights of the precise lust one had
for wire-thin manboys whose jeans fit them
like stovepipes. Their coke and Ritalin habits
a fond memory now, like their screaming.

Love, a pure love (one had) preciousness,
the non-death years, vomit in the men's room,
steaming mopwater and a beer and Slayer loud,
fifty-pound flour bags like blocks of sentiment,
and a favorite kitchen manager's
smile, rough with approval.

One had bad habits and great legs.
One was not merely
youthful...one
was young.

FEBRUARY

Crocus and daffodil already pierce this long nonseason,
as busy people's pleasant lives rustle like bedding
and carry us another day...the earth
does not open up into one horror-hole,
but by pinpoints that twinkle over the map
and seem avoidable.

I fizzle around in my car and imagine I'm better
than the builders of new mansions. What
does it help? It seems normal
I should stop at a convenience store,
whine for an ice-cream bar,
let my boyfriend buy it for me.

People await sacrifice and I do what I can.
Which lies are necessary? I had believed
none were.

THOSE WERE THE DAYS

A mostly sleepless night at Tricia's
looking at her old photos, alone:
her dashing dad at 21 in khakis and oxfords,
her mom like a tiny tanned sea nymph
in a bright green bikini,
a large white baby Tricia
marooned on her lap.

Our lives in the early sixties!
Could we get back there?
Colors were better,
there were all sorts of grandparents standing around
wearing thick black plastic glasses frames.
Men in sharp gray hats wore cigars in their shirt pockets
and dressing-tables had silver brush-and-mirror sets.
Furniture seemed to understand how it stood,
there was no messing around. Everything was recent.

Snap purses opened to metal lipstick tubes
in frightening shades because women had shock value.
Women followed assiduous hair schedules
yet drank rye at parties.
You could have sex with someone in an apartment
listening to a jazz record, and then go to work.
People were shy about their ages.
At a gathering someone might play the piano,
"Stardust Memories," or some Irving Berlin.
People were named Irving. Also Joan.

Now people are named Jennifer and Brad
and it's just awful. And nobody
takes a good picture anymore.

THE WAY TO DO IT

Troubled joints: the leer of aging,
unable not to compare myself to the British actress
we saw last night, despite having no feeling
about it: habit eventually replaces emotion,
isn't that what we see in long marriages?

Here comes the urge to encapsulate,
editorialize, using two example couples
and a wistful bent note at the end:
the representative anecdote:
and here compare yourself to some scholar or poet—

And here, gently upbraid your lover
for comparing himself, fearlessly call out your best friend
for the same, talk about commercials and psycho-messaging,
Fat Art Thin Art, models, remind everybody of famous people's
unhappiness and the inevitable crash of artistic genius á la McCartney,
play "Blackbird" and "Say Say Say" in quick succession
as insurance for driving your point home
to the dullest tone-deaf listener,
the person who'd never notice the bass line in "Paperback Writer"—

and resist the urge to bind it all together
with a self-deprecating drawstring encouraging
a slight morality,
ya fuckin'
control freak.

COUNTRY CLUB

Mom thought we'd have a more boho life.
But we joined the Club, like both sets of grandparents,
and my brother and I were loosed, shaggy &
androgynous, into the tanned raft of rich children.

Ivy covered the chain-link fence on all sides
while black men and women in white jackets
drifted from building to building, and seniors
chugged through the parking lot in golf carts.
I heel-toed the brick path to the Grill
where I could get a perfect chocolate shake
by signing a small pad with my dad's number.
I'd go to the patio alone and suck it slowly,
the blank faces of passing adults unchanging
when they were unable to place me.
But once in a while it would be Mrs. Fisher
or Mr. Taylor, who'd flash a smile and my name,
and briefly I would be seen by a larger world.

At the pool, kids would play Marco Polo,
the thrilling boys I never saw at school
making wild spread-eagle dives
over our reaching hands. Bursting up
from the water, they flung their heads back
to whip their hair in a tangle,
never coming up like seals
the way the girls did.
I wanted to fling my hair too,
but cold dread slowed me
as I approached the surface,
and I came up again face-
first, like a girl.

At swim meets, the older boys screeched
the team's wild monkey call, dumping packets
of dry Kool-Aid into their mouths
for quick energy. They stood
in clumps so close to me: goosefleshed
arms, red and blue tongues, and
rasping, privileged laughter.

I'd hang around in the four feet,
submerging myself for minutes
to hold mermaid poses on the ice-blue floor,
a ten-year-old girl in a yellow bikini
under the silhouettes of boys blocking out the sun.

RECEPTION

The eloped couple submits
to the toast, bulging with drugs.
He/she, cartilage piercings
and teardrop tattoos, s/he h/she, wh/
o, imagining an original life.

Her auburn hair heavy
like floor-length drapery, his gelled
into angry rebellion, dressed in silk
before their families. She laughs and
laughs, her redwine mouth open
like a skeleton. He cuffs people
on the back, speaking
under his breath. He strokes
her spine.

Under her father's stark face,
the party slinks forward,
the four-man rehab blues band
with the twins in it. Mark's
the healthy one. Everybody's got
a flute of champagne but
you and me, everyone goes
to the roof to smoke except
us, what are we waiting for?
When I was young I waited
for you. No more.

LOST SONG

Neither wife nor mother,
I straighten things. Sunday
morning, time for absolution
anyway. I have not been unfaithful
yet this year, that part's over.
There are still college boys
who twitch and shift like antelopes,
there are still deliverymen
who come and go...

I stride through the gallery
hand outstretched, eager to meet
the one behind the rifle.

My dramas swell into balloons
that pinch themselves off
and fade into pinprick anti-stars—
I was I was I was I was

PICK A SCENE

Clipping my nails while you cry on the phone.
Is this the way love ends?

And scenes from a past
fly like bits of tissue from a moving car:
your terrible wet marble eyes in the back lot
screaming white, your white hands waving off
the dry laughing sobs that stopped in my mouth,
and though I had nothing to say I called again and again
while the whole bar murmured shock in the background
and she told me not to call.

Or July, your apartment—your dad dead
and you so beautiful in that yellow Stax shirt.
Is it all not absurd? We lie for hours
under the moon, it's nothing we've ever done.
We've planned to go to the Stax museum,
we've planned a life, an album.
But we've been inside smoking to horror movies.

Which was our real life, that we would have had:
you getting enraged in a restaurant, us singing
George and Melba, gossiping about alcoholic
losers, driving to Nashville in the rain, Elvis
on, you hold me all night & I hold you,
the orange cat mashing into our faces each morning?

Which life was ours? My
Johnny, my love.

1985

I still want to be pretty,
the way I felt in 9th
when you, a senior, glanced down on me
in the BK parking lot
and, later, nibbled my ear
with your long fingers
until I could have mewed helpless baby sounds
had I not been sitting next to my brother
on your lap in the car with all his friends
who kept chorusing "*Myr-tle, Myr-tle,*"
but we drove only as far as Kernersville.

Sex did not exist. I saw you months later
at the Crush Dance, everyone trying to fix you up
with the tallest girl, and we said hi in the hallway once
trying to avoid my brother, we didn't talk again
until *the* last dance, no joke, you actually
came up to me and asked me for it, impossible,
we were standing on the floor of that old gym
barely moving inside your hands—

and I was lucky, you skinny fool,
because the next time
after the prom after-party at Grace's
I got special permission for, we defied
my furious brother as we split up at dawn
and I rode in your parents' boat of a car
with your arm around me and the immense front seat
falling away on the other side, light peeking
into the sky while Hunter and Julie groped silently
behind us, you drove calm as an adult to the street
in front of my house, and turned to me
with the whole year on our lips
while hymns blasted from the sedan's old radio.

SUMMER HOLIDAY

A damp wish to be seduced
dissolves like sugar in the hot herb tea
that replaces coffee when one's system
rejects the harsher, beloved beverage.

How old are you now? One's thoughts suggest
with the kind of hopeless smile
you might see on a middle-aged doctor
who's just been cleaned out in a malpractice suit.

The abstract number
floats in state, suspended in a liquid chamber
in the core of the body, which strangely
looks better than ever.

The potentialities
of the thirty-two-year-old body
stream in all directions, like the Moravian star.

The woman at thirty-two
has not been ruined, the bland flesh of her youth
having striated and lengthened
along with her previously blunt thoughts
into a saltier whole—who'd have
thought such a thing could happen
to that round-eyed Christian Daisy May
one used to be?

The woman
at thirty-two
has not been ruined.
Her opportunities
have shifted, in some cases
to some really great thing
or other.

89.3

> *So if you hear me on the radio, just sing along*
> *'cause I know that you forget me when the music's gone,*
> *But honey you inspired my last six songs,*
> *and all I can think of is you...*
> —J.H., Jr.

Full of solitary certainty, you navigate towards coffee
this morning, radio snapped on. Driver's side window cracked,
a/c on 1 to cut the humidity, you're in red plaid
with a decent tan and haircut, tumble-drying points
in the mind: check teeth. Bicyclist is annoying. Roll and fruit.

In the store, what should cross anyone's mind
among infinite choice. Soft faces chomp gently,
softening eggs and pancakes. At some moment today
you will be disappointed.

As you cross the white-hatched crosswalk
to your car (left open) picturing the man
you left three months ago, cars slow for you.
He had practice last night, he'll be in bed still.
What else would happen, when you get in
and crank the engine, but his voice
flooding the car, bigger than God?

There is never anything
to be remembered, because events
simply fix themselves in time.
Down the road someone sleeps
in a two-room apartment, and if we take the minicam
through the open window where the cat-door is,
we see you are not there.

The song lumbers forward
on the molasses conduit of his voice
through "your" ride home.
Everything is yours now,
the way you wanted it.

CELEBRITY

Were it a crisp morn in LA,
I would be in that crap grocery
buying a bag of prepackaged gorp
and, with ostentation at the register,
scorning the wall of fitness and fame mags
where Jadas and Marnies, Winonas and Brads
froze across their famous lives like hood ornaments.
I, the Ann of flannel and elastic, never wanted fame.

Though it weights the tongue
like a chocolate diet candy, wanting equally
to be swallowed and spit out.

Those Ellayers with their bitchin yoga practices
I'd be, had I stayed. Had I stayed in Cali-for-nyah,
plowing the sidewalk with clunky-chunk sandals,
I'd be drinking martinis with very very smart guys
at coppertop bars, reading their screenplays
with a bludgeoned interest and a silver bowl
full of *objet d'art* matchbooks.

That was John Travolta, would be said,
and I against my will would be affected,
carried backward to my first home
where the fat, luminous basement TV
kaleidoscoped my mind forward into a Bronx high school
where he was stopped forever in perfect youth.

When you're rich, or dead, you can go back there,
and observe the way you ought to want to, un-
observed, because right now you can't decide
whether you want to see or be seen. Most people
can't. So, do you still think you're better than them?
Just because you don't know who Russell Crowe is?

AUGUST

Midday: a bright blue sky films over;
I remember our life together.

You can either decide it's small-town bullshit
or choose to feel loss again and again—

we both choose the latter.
My tree, you would just be waking,

climbing over me from the bad side
of the bed, while I read some terrible

Houdini biography. You pee loudly
in the bowl, and on the way back always

always stop in front of the mirror,
your sparse hair all funny. You fix it

and pick up the phone to check missed calls.
I put the bio down on the carpet

amid small gray drifts of dust.
You brush while I shower,

handle me as I dry and dress.
A new person's more exciting

but you aren't new
as you once were to me.

STORK

Your face is an unfamiliar bird
coming towards me in strong light

while old love plays its repeat track
on and on in my heart.

You are not my tree
the lyrics would say

if they knew any better.
You are a strange stork

that flaps around,
dipping your neck

to peck me here and there.
The human being is unused

to the fitful movements
of the bird. The human

has worshipped the bird
in varying cultures:

the phoenix, the eagle.
But the white awkward stork

has not held its image
in stone or soft metal,

has not been fallen upon.
We've kept him trundled

away, we only want one thing
from him: babies, wrapped in blue, or pink.

A MONTH OF MONDAYS

Bright harsh wintry light and things,
this Monday morning in November.
Such arbitrariness.

I walked away from a good man who loved me,
but who hasn't? Now, I wait
in the unflinching light of your gaze

while days check themselves off.
June July August.
We lazily haggle film choices,

wake early and part.
I don't have time for anything.

~ ~ ~

Your mother screams your name
and you roll your eyes at me
She wants everything

You're a grown-up American boy,
you can do what you want.
In the car I sit next to you

and I'm a good trooper,
I can do a lot of things,
help you garbage-pick shelving and

display cases, look hot at racetracks.
I'm an asset, I never scream, I'm
nothing like her, of course.

STRIPPER

I was so drunk yesterday
by early evening I had forgotten
the pain of the stripper who gets sent home
because she's too old and burnt out.

I smelled like underarm sweat
and cigarettes because I was so drunk
I took that old pack from Claire
and sat on the porch chain-smoking

the way I thought I was finished with forever.
Today I sip a travel mug full of hot water
brushing my teeth every hour
to get rid of it.

And the pain I feel is the pain of the stripper
whose body was too worn down,
and it's the next day and she's in her apartment
remembering their abashed, rigid faces.

Twenty years ago she could have had any one
of them without effort. And now they are
simply different, too different from her,
they imagine. They get drawn out

of their fantasy. There's too much:
her leathered tan, collapsing mouth,
the way the makeup sits on her face,
you think of death and mothers.

The old stripper puts away last night's thong
and titty-covers. If she gets them out
again, it will be because someone
is calling her, wanting her.

VEIL

Even the warm pictures of last night lose detail by ten:
peanut soup with the girls, and I'm rushing around
trying to keep the puppy from the table
in four conversations, Claire & Sammy breaking up
again, Ali's depression, Roberta's granite opinions.

Who I was amid that group: the maximized wife,
next-to-be-married, the spinster
who just hasn't realized it yet...oh, girls
and their wedding plans, or their still-shocking decision
to avoid the whole mess: it's still the center
of a female life. *Are you married?*

In a lower cabinet of a breakfront,
the yellow spider of my mother's veil
crouched in a thirty-year meditation
on its one splendid day.

Had we asked it for help, it would've said
wait, wait,
it would have whispered.

HOLIDAYS

For you, I'd like to wear black angora earmuffs
and a see-through nightie, but I don gray sweatpants instead
and stuff my head with those hot pink foam plugs,
because it's cold and the heater clanks.

It's winter, we're at your place,
the land of bony embraces and cheap food.
We stuff ourselves into the sofa
to watch video-copied super-8s.
Your dad appears like a heavy bird,
running with you and your brother in the yard;
like a father, he lets you win.

Two years ago, Claire slammed into his six-five ghost
in this basement—and even you, the skeptic,
believe it. It's easy to believe
your father will come back for you.

CHRISTMAS DAY

In a world sickened with celebrity,
I would echo Scrooge's claim,
I am not who I was…

But who would listen
to a damn
white woman

the speck inside
an invisible ball
of personal space

whizzing by homeless veterans
with a small inconclusive smile,
wine bottles clanking in the back seat

like Marley's chains.
Oh, Christ, the need
to *talk* about it—

throwing snowballs
of money
at easy targets.

Two

INDEPENDENCE DAY, 2002

This morning, the flags don't need to be retrieved from dank cabinets and unfolded in a vague ritual, two Americans standing at either end. The flags are already out, they've been out for ten months, buttressed by tiny sticker-flags, rhinestone lapel pins, kicky swizzle-stick flags for the pencil mug at work. The flags have been living outside, moving around, they're getting used to it. They've been slapping against the force of our ideas, and swelling.

The nylon weave of the flag, chunked through a machine in Southeast Asia, remains tight. An irreducible pleasure results from the flag worn on the body, blood and Union troops swirled around the milky torsos of American citizens, snug enough to feel like safety.

The President comes on like a lightbulb in the public mind. His thin lips curl around Arabic names, his sense of things keen as an eagle. After he steps down from the podium, an aide brings him a miniature pecan pie, and he opens the crackly plastic and bites happily with his new high-res tongue and teeth. To him, nothing's ever tasted so good.

LESSON IN ADULTHOOD

Waking up to adult life, stone in the jaw.
You'll never be mirrored by your father

again...what of it? Now is the time
to drive to work, to snap on the news

or let some other adult's teeth
grind into your neck—let's get over this

as grownups. Pop a beer, measure up
some gin and vermouth, make it sloppy.

Perc up a pot of coffee, extend a cigarette,
let a hand dangle out a car window

but don't let your kids do it.
Get a cardiogram.

Breast self-exam, pelvic, regular
dental, hair and nails. Keeping up

with the decaying human form
takes a lot of experts.

Get one to teach you how to come, for fuck's sake,
before your bunged-up female equipment

dies childless, you know? If you can't manage
to create a life to nurture, you could at least get

over yourself enough to offer some guy
the sight of you conquered, helpless.

SUE ANN COURT

Was anything any different today?
A couple of cigarettes with Kimo,
talk of relationships.

His head in the dull blue midday
a warm cubic shape
balanced like an ice cream.

Rarely, we seem or feel graceful.
His movements remind me of placing small objects
on a shelf, and somehow colors

focus themselves forward as if
they, too, would like to be seen
by him.

Because Kimo because.
Your light hangs from the ceiling,
you find your way through,

your mouth a neat dumpling
I'll never chew...a mouth notices
a laugh, and takes it for a ride.

These are the other uses of mouths
pillows for dying words
but that's so tragic, so urban,

that I'll admit I didn't say it
and credit an ex-boyfriend,
and Kimo doesn't mind,

nobody minds, while the white spring
of middle winter slides by
like a kid on a sled.

REFLECTIONS IN A BLUE EYE

I have a certain certainty
I can no longer see—
a fist closes in on itself,
hurting no one but itself.

I think of her anger
running all over her like fake wind.
Her hair flying like a witch's,
bright blue light on her face.

She was damaged, like a mop.
And she told you all about it
until the shape of her teeth
(small, pointy) startled

a dormant malevolence
and you began to press her
slowly, slowly,
out of significance.

Wearing a gray hat she tries
turning on the charm, it's sad
because you can't look
and you know she wants you to;

sad because judgment crawls
over her like a tarantula, sad as a dead
fucking bird, it's that fucking sad.
If there ever was love between you.

NOTICE

Brightness and unceasing wind, hey ho,
and the marriages of convenient friends
in high spring, credit cards ablaze.

Young American adult, whose purpose
was once the world's envy, now a shaggy
indistinction, earning minimum wage

in a bright spring, alive
as any third-world farmer.
Into this background

my complaints are shouted
and forgotten: *shallow people
stupid presidents*

*my boyfriend forgot about me,
I want a baby now.*
The wedding guests move

uncertainly on the pitched cement floor.
Everybody wanted a drink
when they got here.

I had a bourbon & ginger
and stood in the cold grass as a witness,
not as a friend but as a girlfriend,

and noticed several people from a
peripheral past, and how meaning
had thinned, and noticed

my enduring arrogance.
Which makes all the wars
in other places possible.

JEALOUSY

Some girl, some generic girl
with a baseball hat
your man had before
you—a square-faced girl
with a busting bod,
rhinocerous nose,
honey-brown mustache.

How unkind you are
to the past, as if the future
needs your vote
to succeed. Any idiot
with a C-minus average
(such as she had) could tell
just by observing you observing
the past with such interest,
that you're in trouble now...

Who's ever benefited
from your hindsight?

Yet, my land, she was the sunburn queen,
queen of the darkness and orange tie-dye,
a braided hippie-queen in rimless spectacles
tapping formulae into her computer.

She had a life, and her life split off,
and she continues somewhere
in her honey-blond twenties,

and she wouldn't know you
if you blasted a hole
straight through the ground.

SUPERSTAR

These perfect days all in a row
mean I should imitate somebody.
I should have a second, third life,
no one should imitate me.

My stale annoyance at everybody
forms a dry-toast border to life.
Observe insects, or something,
fatten yourself on oils.

Vivid recollections fade into a schedule.
Dreams no longer populate themselves
with anything or anyone worth mentioning:
last night, for example, Bruce Springsteen.

This to me would indicate
a dying imagination, a shortcut
to knowing the unknown.
Sex with Bruce was the dream's promise.

Someone who believes in art
should see the red flag here.
Because anyone, really, knows the difference
between a fucking a star
and having your own mind.

AISLE

There's no escape I really want
from the world's newest evil,
so it has already changed me

at the entranceway of Lowe's
where bodies pile higher
and higher
behind the cashier's blue smock.

I could have wanted better
but I stand in Lowe's
with the other lovers of convenience,
running our eyes absently
over magazines.

I could have done more
than slide along the smooth concrete
of these passageways slowly,
as though out of life,
with a dull focus fixed
on the next item:
spline, net, glass, rods of pure wood
run through a circular saw.

Stunning ununiqueness,
reminding us of hate,
reminding us of why we came here.

JESUS STOPS IN

There's a new Jesus on the scene, y'all—
the tortured body, intense eyes etc.
White ribs stitched with
small smooth black hairs;
female note in the laugh
of a male mouth—get a load
of this delicious stuff, y'all—
and enough of it to go around.

His smell the smell of smooth sand,
he tastes of cigarette ends
and undisturbing dreams.
He seems not to mind
the fist in the sky, the exhausting anger
unloaded minute by minute
into the sun—don't tell anyone
you found such a living
fish, lightning rod, salty loaf.

Jesus in the elevator, Jesus on the floor,
Jesus at your house, drinking down
a white rum mojito
among the Buddhists.
Lie still and let him
open your jaw, dig your fingers
into his back, like a rack
of light wood, & let him carry you
down this long river a little while.

HOPE

I know that I love James Carville
just as right now I know I love you,
and there are so many gorgeous quiet Saturdays before us
we will spend together or separately in the dead clean leaves
that fall towards the end of September, when children feel
a delicious impatience for cold nights we no longer feel
but in the flash ghosts of ourselves we sometimes pass through
such nights—fall arrives like this, for us. And whether or not
we are James Carville, or love him, as I know I do,
we experience the sharpness of what we do not feel
in miniscule bursts that shock through our thicknesses
like a flashbulb. James, I never imagined this adult life,
or you crowing through it in your birdy way—where
were you? I needed you so, you yokel, so indescribably
that I was incapable of imagining your face,
roundly crowded with thought, tipped towards its center
like a mashed penny. You are so smart, so smart
and so impatient I lean on the thought of you,
I rest my head on the thought of your middle back
like a sturdy corduroy pillow. I love you.
And I'm certain I will never get over it.